Also By Russ Mitchell:

Personal Improvement:

Basic Body Mechanics For Martial Artists
Driving With Ease
The Weightless Ribbon: Rolling With Ease In Seven Lessons
Klutz Therapy
Spaceman Fitness (forthcoming)
Fighter's Friend (forthcoming)

Fiction:

Malik The Pawn
Malik Unbound
The Sunset World (forthcoming)

Fencing:

Fencing at the Theresian Academy (orig. published 1886)
Sir Gusztáv Arlow's *Sabre Fencing* (orig. published 1902)
Hungarian Hussar Sabre and Fokos Fencing
Sabre Fencing, by Károly Leszák (orig. published 1906)
Franco-Japanese Military Sabre and Bayonet
Sabre Fencing in High Tierce (orig. published 1894)

Stage Combat:

How to (Look) Kick(-)Ass with Swords

To everybody who was picked last in sports...

but had fun anyway.

KLUTZ THERAPY

simple habits that can change your life

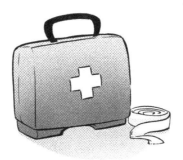

RUSS MITCHELL

PICTURES BY KAT LAURANGE

ISBN: 9798394146640

Cover Art and Design by Kat Laurange

TABLE OF CONTENTS

INTRODUCTION. OR, "THEY'RE COMING TO TAKE ME AWAY, HAHA-OWCH!"

When I was a kid my Mom lived in terror of CPS (Child Protective Services) coming to take my brother and I away. It wasn't that my folks were doing any of the hideous and awful things that usually result in CPS showing up. But it LOOKED like it, because my twin and I were just FESTOONED with bruises. And if asked why we were covered in bruises, we just said "we're clumsy."

(cue alarms from everybody who's ever worked with abused kids)

But the truth of the matter is, we were THAT clumsy. Banging into the coffee table hard enough to rattle the walls? Well, that's just how we walked through rooms! We weren't just a mess — — we were covered in the kinds of disturbing bruises that prompted worried queries of *"how did you get THAT?!"* And the answer was usually that we had *no idea*.

So one day my twin brother and I were watching a television show with Russian ballet dancers and he said "I just realized. The ballerinas are graceful because they know where their bodies are."

For a pair of somewhat sickly and seriously clumsy teenagers, this was a bolt from the blue (enough that I remember the exact wording almost forty years later). It wasn't a shock that ballerinas knew where their bodies were... but that they were even CAPABLE of knowing where their bodies were. This was a thing? What kind of dark magic lets you know where you are in space? We were amazed and a little bit awed at the world opening up in front of us.

So thirty years later, fencers come to me as their "body mechanics guru," I've written a booklet for martial artists and their coaches, and I'm generally considered a reasonably nimble and fluidly-moving guy.   No professional dancer, mind you, especially after the hilarious laundry list of training-related injuries I picked up over thirty years of fighting, but I generally qualify as "moves well." Because of that, I've ALSO talked to a lot of people who have said some version of "Oh, I want to stop being a klutz, but I'm totally not trusting you on this because you're one of THEM -- one of those people who knows where his body is." (That is absolutely totally how that convo went).

But the simple truth is, not only have I "been there" as a klutz, but you'd have had to be far side of the moon level klutzy to match the heavy bruising and constantly-broken mugs and bowls and anything-else not made of plastic as I grew up.

If I could learn to move better, you can, too. And with thirty years of thinking really hard about it, I can show you how to do it easily and without scheduling in a single extra hour for "exercise."

That sounds WAY too good to be true, right?

The problem with improving is that Improving is change, and *you can't change and stay the same.* So how can I show you how to get a lot less klutzy without investing a lot of time you don't have for doing a brand new workout program?

Well, unfortunately, there really is no free lunch. You'll have to pay your way in somehow. And in this case, "somehow" will mean....

1. Reading a little bit of this awesomely short and easy-to-understand booklet and looking at Kat's cute doodles.

2. Playing with the ideas you read, paying attention to how you feel while doing a bunch of stuff you ALREADY have to do... but doing them in a slightly different way.

3. Keeping it gentle so you don't hurt yourself.

That's it. After a little while of doing it, you then ask yourself "hey, self, this new way of doing things is different. What's up with that, and what do I think about it?"

Somewhere along the line, you'll have changed your habits, and how you do things will have changed ever so slightly for the better. It will happen simply because you paid attention to it.

You may not wind up doing the thing you read quite the way I do. In fact, you almost certainly *won't* do them the way I do. You have a different body, living a different life, in a different home, sitting on different furniture, yadda yadda. It would be really weird if you read the next section and thought "YES, I WILL DO EXACTLY WHAT IS WRITTEN HERE ON THE VERY FIRST TRY!"

I mean, let's be serious. How do you know if the new habits are actually safe and good for you yet?

If things seem hard or weird or discouraging, don't fret or beat yourself up. After all, you've lived your entire live without this book. And you've still managed to stay alive! Go you! Little tiny baby steps are fine. In fact, little tiny baby steps are BEST, because they're safe and easy and take *almost no effort*. This stuff is like saving a penny a day, only it comes with a MONSTER of an interest rate in your favor. As a bonus, since it takes almost no effort to do these things, there's no "do I really want to do this stuff TODAY?" Effortless doesn't cost much!

So let the pennies add up. Over the next few weeks, then months, and then yes, finally, years, you'll notice that it's just easier and happier to be you. And that's the point, right?

Russ Mitchell and Kat Laurange,
May 2023

WAKING: GET SOME FLOPPY-FEET!

BEEP BEEP BEEP BEEP!

My wife is a morning person. She doesn't want to be -- given a chance, she sleeps in til the crack of noon. But most of the time, she doesn't have that chance, and she needs lots of extra time to become a fully-functional human being. So her alarm always goes off "early-ish."

That's great for me. I have mastered the *secret kung fu art* of lying in bed until thirty seconds before it's time to go... and then magically appearing at the front door tapping my toe impatiently for everybody to get the lead out and hop in the car.

(I'm pretty sure my wife is exaggerating on this a bit, but it means I get to lie in bed an extra fifteen minutes like a lump that really doesn't want to move and which thinks going "*mrmph*" constitutes carrying on a conversation.)

The lump wiggles its feet every which way in order to wake up. First wriggling the toes, then the foot, then the other foot, then back and forth like working a sewing machine or an old-timey car with a clutch, the works. It takes about a minute, and when I do that before I get up, my back is a LOT less stiff, and I have more of a bounce in my step.

IT CAN'T POSSIBLY BE THAT EASY. I WANT MY MONEY BACK

Actually, there's some sophisticated things going on here. When there's pressure on the bottom of your foot, a seriously technical reflex we won't get into here sends a signal up to your hips and spine saying "hey, a surface! I need to be standing on that, or else I'm probably going to smack the back of my head on something hard! I should maximize my contact with said surface!"

You can also, as you wriggle your feet, think of letting excess tension go away.

For example, when you get to your ankle, there's a portion of your wiggle that's taking your heel further from your backside (the "pull your toes up" part), and a portion where you bring it closer (the "flappy feet" part). In order to "pull your toes up," your calf has to get slightly longer and more relaxed. It's built into a process the movement nerds call "reciprocal inhibition," and it happens automagically™.

So while you wiggle your ankle, if you focus on the part that involves relaxing the calves, you get better and better at loosening them up. And if you focus on relaxing the front of your shins when your toes go long in the same process, you get better at relaxing those muscles, too. That means you get out of bed with a lot of your joints looser and more comfortable, with notably better circulation, and you get into the habit of getting out of bed with your joints ever so slightly more comfortable than the day before.

But by wriggling your feet while lying flat in bed, you also put your feet in the positions they'll be inhabiting for most of the day, which wakes up your hips and pelvis, *without any weight attached.* You could do the same thing in a pool -- except for the effort involved with all that "not drowning" business. You get to make little movements that loosen up your hips while still letting them slack off in bed for an extra minute or two.

It's nice for me, but it's REALLY nice if you're the one who has to get up first. Because once your feet DO hit the ground, your joints are already wide-awake and ready to face the day.

TRICKY BONUS FOR OVER-ACHIEVERS:

1. How much of your body can you get to come along for the ride when you foot-wiggle?

2. How far up your body can you feel the wiggling as you focus on moving by letting go of tension, rather than moving-by-tightening?

3. And what changes if you make super-small "my toes are spies and don't want to attract predatory housecats" wiggles that are so small nobody knows you're even doing them?

The toes must die.

FIRST THINGS FIRST:
TEETH YOUR BRUSH!

So remember: the basic principle of this book is that you're going to greatly improve your quality of life *without* having to add in extra gym trips and workout routines.

That will mean learning to do some things differently, and this is one of them. I have recommended this "Very Dumb Thing" to dozens of clients and students, to rave reviews. So brace yourself – we're not going to do more.

We're going to do DIFFERENTLY.

When your sleepy self heads to the bathroom in the morning to do your "First things" business, brushing your teeth is on that list. (I hope. Because otherwise, you know, EWW?).

The simple act of brushing your teeth can be very difficult for somebody who has tennis elbow or bad arthritis. It's a "distal" activity, which is a fancy way of saying that it's organized from your limbs rather than from the center of your body.

That means that brushing your teeth, humble activity that it is, can actually be a strain for a lot of people. It's a great example of a thing that has to happen, but which isn't doing much good for us besides achieving its intended task.

But what if there was a way to turn it into something that helped wake you up? What if getting your teeth clean could wake you up *and* gradually begin to erase years of neck and back strain while you're at it?

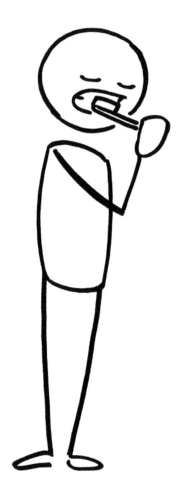

As opposed to the usual barely-awake method.

So here's what you're going to do. Instead of pumping your arm to move the brush around in your mouth, you're going to turn your mouth from side to side while allowing the brush to stay still.

And then you're going to tilt your head so you can get to those "hard to reach places," getting the tops and bottoms and fronts and backs of all your toofies.

That's right. You're not brushing your teeth.

You're teething your brush.

WHY ON EARTH WOULD I WANT TO DO THAT?

The thing is, "teething your brush" takes the same amount of time but is *much* better for you than brushing your teeth. It helps you to use the weight of your head to help loosen up your neck and upper spine, while teaching you how everything from your chest on up can change shape.

And that is important. Relaxing your neck, shoulders, and chest not only improves your balance and overall mobility (you turn your head a *lot*, because, you know, *looking at things*), but it also improves your breathing, and hence, your mood. It's the perfect(ly odd) way to start your day.

MORNING: A SINKING FEELING (IN THE SHOWER)

So sooner or later, you have to wash your knees, right?

For me, showers are a morning thing. I do all my best thinking with a lot of hot water pounding on my neck. Well, maybe not ALL my best thinking: the "pecan pie in a bowl of Fruit Loops, strawberry a la mode" experiment was a Shower Thought, too... but I digress.

But sooner or later you gotta wash your feet, and unless you have a tub that's wide enough to *lounge gloriously* while you do it, that means bending over. So how can you bend over to wash your legs and your feet without your back saying "hello, I have declared that I shall hate you this week?"

Looking down is actually super-interesting, because on the one hand, "ooh, toenail polish!" And on the other hand, your brain says "I am fragile. No splat me like grapefruit, pleaserino." So how can you satisfy both demands? (and make no mistake, the latter is a DEMAND. Your body will sacrifice EVERYTHING, your precious lower back included, to feel sure that your brain is safe from slip-crash-smack).

Well, if you put your hands to your ears and listen carefully, you can now hear all the really fit yoga instructors shouting "hip hinge!, *Hip Hinge!*" But if you easily hip hinge in the shower to wash your feet even when it's just after or just before bed... you may not really be a klutz. I mean, thanks for buying this book, and there's still stuff here that can help you, but we're going to pitch this part of your day less at "is actually a yoga instructor" and more at "I can touch my toes (without aspirin) if I bend my legs and I'm *really careful* about it."

Let's start with your head. It's like having an eight to twelve pound bowling ball balanced on top of a five or six foot stick (assuming you're neither a hobbit nor a basketball player). When you tilt your head from side to side, that weight matters, and your body fires up the muscles to keep you erect. Not just your neck muscles, either. Muscles from your toes to your nose fire off. AH-OOOH-GAH! AH-OOOH-GAH! SHE'S BENDING OVER, ALERT, ALERT!

Oh, those poor hamstrings!.

But. If you bend from your lower back and wash your toes that way, that takes a lot of flexibility. Your hips CAN do it (if you're not injured), but now you have two poles (your legs and your torso) and your head's at the end of the second one. You're balancing your ten pound bowling ball (your head) a couple of feet away from your base of support -- the feet you're trying to wash in the first place.

It's a lot simpler and easier if you can keep your head pretty much over top of your feet while you wash. And then you don't *need* to be "a super-bendy person," because every part of you is only going to have to bend or stretch a little bit.

The alternative is using the very bottom of your lower back to do all the work.

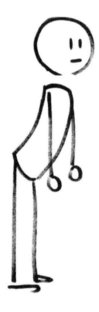

Bending like this is work. A LOT of work.

So try this instead. You're going to slowly and gently bend down with the intention of keeping your head as close to your body as possible. And if that means that your knees bend, your spine or backside moves backwards, or anything also happens to make foot-washing easy, well.... GREAT!

WHY IS THIS A THING?

When you bend over and keep your head close to you, you bend from the top down with lots of vertebrae, not just one or two.

Head closer to feet means less effort!

So you get to spread the load out to your entire spine, not just the bottom lumbar vertebra where peoples' backs have a tendency to go "oww- oh no!". That means that by the time you've bent down far enough to reach your knees, you're still getting lots of support from half your spine -- the half that's barely bent yet. You only unstack your spine as much as you need to in order to bend. And on the way up, it's just the opposite -- you rise by stacking all your vertebrae one on top of the other, rather than hauling on just the part of your lower back where your pelvis stops and your back begins (or, again, hip hinge-ing if you're on Team Superflexy™).

Meanwhile, your head may be going forwards, but parts of your back and pelvis are going *behind you*. That helps to balance you and make it easier to BEND DOWN, rather than BENDING OVER. And THAT is the big secret that the yoga instructors and gymnasts know -- by taking part of you backwards and part of you forwards, it's easier to balance, and a heck of a lot less work.

THE IMPORTANT PART!

DON'T DO THIS "FOR REPS" LIKE YOU'RE AT THE GYM.

(okay, I mean, ONCE, go for it... but be careful, right?)

All you need is to do it twice a day -- once for each leg. I mean, you have to wash those suckers anyway, right? Having an actual goal that needs to be achieved tells your nervous system "hey, I need results here," and makes it easier, even if you only do "one rep" per day like Archibald Stinky-Leg Jones. Two reps a day will help you learn how to balance yourself and to keep your feet nice and shiny while, *most importantly*, not throwing your back out every time you bend down to get something out of the fridge.

GOING PLACES:
EASY TAI CHI WHILE YOU DRIVE

Note for city-slickers: if you've never driven a day in your life because you live in a place where investing in a car is just total economic nonsense, you can still benefit -- a lot! -- by playing with the same ideas while holding a cup of coffee, a saucepan, or a basket of laundry. Driving is a REALLY good example of how this works, but it's not the only one.

You made it to Chapter Four! Yay! You deserve a drink and so do I. (Hey, this book isn't writing itself.) I'm going to go with a big cup of tea for my "good job, now keep writing so your illustrator doesn't hurt you with a cartoon axe" bonus treat. So now that you have YOUR beverage, raise it up for drinking and stop.

Dramatic recreation of a typical workplace AXE-ident

Look at your elbow.

Is it below your drink when you hold it in the air? Is your elbow to the right side of your drink, or your left side? If you're a righty like me, and your elbow is way over to the left, that may look weird (this is how I made my Mom laugh), but there's no right or wrong. Just drink your drink, and when you have that moment of "I must inevitably have done this all wrong and MUST try new and exciting elbow positions...." do that!

While you're lifting a (somewhat) heavy object in the air repeatedly, what elbow angle makes your shoulders work harder? And at which angle does your shoulder have to work the least? You could, if you were really motivated, hold your shoulder while you played with it, to feel how tense the sides of your shoulder are in each position.

For most of us, that angle is more or less "elbow points STRAIGHT down." That's why tai chi masters constantly harass their more senior students to point their elbows down rather than off to the side, where their shoulders have to work harder than they should be (but they point them down very slowly. So very, VERY slowly.)

So now, next time you get in the car, because that's probably how you get to work, put your hands "at 10 and 2" on the steering wheel and look at where you've put your elbows.

Then try letting your shoulders soften until they point straight down, or closer to it than usual. If you're heavy-chested and sit really close to the steering wheel, *literally* straight down could be a challenge, but you have to drive anyway, so it's still worth playing with. You like relaxed shoulders, right?

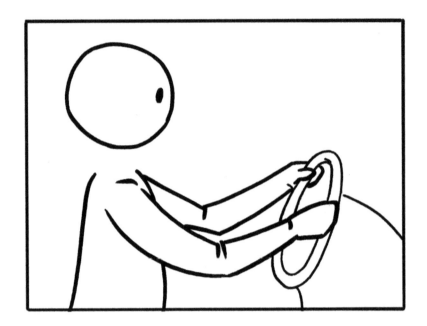

What will then happen is that you have to move the steering wheel, keeping your elbows down, and that will gradually train you to do some magical things:

1. Turn left by coordinating the fall of your left elbow with the rise of the right and vice-versa. That coordination loosens up your chest and ribs.

2. Look left and right while keeping your hands on the wheel by letting your shoulders turn just like your neck does (saving a lot of neck strain!)

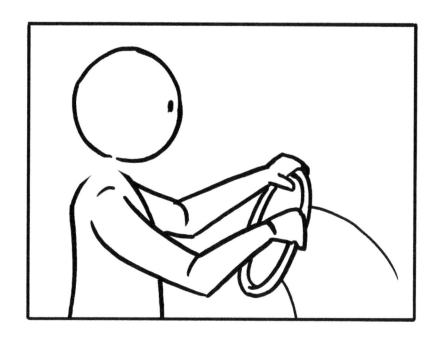

Remember teething your brush?

What __else__ moves when you steer?

3. BONUS. Your hands are now on the wheel, one foot is on the gas, and one foot is either standing, or else on the little foot-rest thingy. That means that all your driving now has to come from the big muscles in your torso, and because you know how to drive, it will come EASILY from your torso (or 'core,' if you like the term). So you're literally training yourself to move better in *and* out of the car while you drive.

The truly amazing part of all this is that just by changing one or two little habits while you drive, you'll start to stay a LOT looser behind the wheel. You can even drive the kids to grandma's house three or four hours away and not feel horribly stiff when you get out of the car. In essence, you'll have been doing tai chi all the way to work and back every day, and slowly and gently massaging those ribs and aching back muscles out of "sack of painful wet concrete" to "okay, I just drove six hours, but does anybody want to go walk to the coffee shop?"

It won't come overnight. But if you drive this way and pay attention to where you point your elbows, you'll get softer and looser and you'll feel a LOT better when you get where you're going. Which is probably to work, and I've never met a Boss who wasn't happier when people come into work smiling.

Plus, you've got to drive (or drink coffee) anyway, so why not use that to help improve yourself?

DON'T LET THE CUBE KILL YOU: OR, SILKY SPINE SITTING

So if you're like a lot of people reading this, at least part of your day is spent sitting for a living. But how do you sit?

Did you read this and just "sit up straight?"

Stop that! That's exhausting! If it weren't exhausting, everybody would sit like that, all the time.

But sitting "like a cashew," as a colleague of mine likes to call it, isn't all that great, either. Sitting slumped all day is terrible for your back, awful for your neck, and worse for your mood. It makes people sluggish, lethargic, and often depressive and de-motivated. Plus it's not all that great for your breathing, either, because of the way it squishes your diaphragm and prevents it from moving smoothly.

So if slumping is terribad, but sitting up straight is torture, no wonder everybody's solution to the problem trends either towards "just ignore it and hope for the best," or else "buy a really expensive chair and *then* hope for the best."

So what can we do?

Try this.

Sit in your chair and roll forwards and backwards right where your butt meets the cushion, until you find the sweet spot where you're at your most "effortlessly tall."

If you do that, you'll notice something really, really cool. It becomes a lot easier to smile. You may even start smiling spontaneously and making your co-workers wonder what you're up to.

HOW'S IT WORK?

In some respects, "posture" is all about how much your head weighs, which you can't do much about, and how you balance that weight over the rest of you, which is very much under your control. Sitting is basically just "standing, but on your backside rather than your feet."

> It's not an accident that we keep coming back to „how to balance the weight of your head."

When you roll your butt forwards and backwards in the chair, you're changing how far forwards or backwards the contact point between your pelvis and your chair is. That changes how you balance your head, relative to your backside.

If you roll backwards in your chair, you'll start to slump, because the alternative is to lean backwards with a straight back, at which point the weight of your head has you way off balance and your whole nervous system says „EEK! EMERGENCY EMERGENCY AHHH! WE'RE GOING TO CRASH!"

This is very important, because you really don't want to hit the back of your head onto a hard surface. That can kill you, and is literally a leading cause of fall fatalities. So it's much more comfortable, if you roll backwards, to let your spine bend so that the back of your head (that is, the heavy part!) is safely over top of your backside again.

And then you're sitting like a cashew.

If you try to straighten your spine vertically from this position, it's a lot of work and doesn't feel very good at all: you're overworking the heck out of your back muscles.

The alternative is to go so far forwards that you either have to look forwards the floor (not very productive unless you're tying your shoes), or else to arch your spine backwards to get your head, once again, closer to being over your backside and in balance. Just like hunching, this also makes your back work much too hard, and some people *do* sit like this all day (but a lot fewer than those who hunch).

So your back isn't the culprit here. It's the victim, doing its level best to keep your head where it needs to be for your convenience and your safety. If you check your position and sense for when you're working the least, but yet also are tallest, you'll probably find that you're a little further forwards of where you usually sit (usually about an inch in front of your "sit bones," depending on your build). The back of your head will be over top of your pelvis, and sitting up straight becomes easy. In the process, breathing gets easier, too. And that helps your mood.

The mental effort of getting used to that will take a bit, of course. But you'll breathe more easily, you'll smile more, and you won't have the "I've been sitting for eight hours blahs" that makes you feel listless for an hour after you get home from work. The muscular effort of sitting in balance is so much less than what you have to do when you slump, that eventually you won't *want* to slump. Squashing your midsection won't feel relaxed any more – it'll feel, well, *squashed.* And when you do lean back, you'll do it differently, and better, because it'll be a choice you can play around with rather than being the only way you know how to sit.

WASHING YOUR P'S AND Q'S

Quick question: how many times per day do you wash your hands?

If you're a little person with a seemingly professional talent for getting your grubby mitts dirty, muddy, and every mother's favorite, *sticky*, the answer is probably "nowhere near enough."

For most of the rest of us, let's say that we wash our hands at a "healthy hygiene minimum" of five times a day unless we're out camping or we eat lunch on a job site where washing up ahead of time isn't an option.

Try this: next time you're washing up, have your right foot a bit backwards and your left forwards, and instead of washing by pumping your elbows, lift your right heel off the ground, rotating your body from your right foot to push and pull your right hand forwards and backwards across your left hand while you wash. You can play with which foot is back and which hand is active as much as you feel like (a few extra moments washing up is probably a good thing). In doing so, it looks like you're moving your hands, but you're *actually* turning your hips and shoulders while letting your arms go along for the ride.

It's better if the ball of your foot doesn't twist and turn on the floor while you do, but if that's hard, let your foot just do whatever it needs to do for this to stay easy and comfortable. After doing this for a while, you'll notice that you'll walk faster, and when you need to run, that gets easier, too. Plus, people may be telling you that you seem taller lately.

WAIT, WHAT?

This is a fun one. You have to wash your hands. But by doing it this way, you're also practicing some really important physical skills that will make almost everything you do in life easier.

Washing the „normal" way, all movement from the
extremities -- but your body held still.

When you walk, you pick up one leg and swing the other to put it down in front of the standing leg. Seems obvious, right? But in order to do that, you first have to put all your weight into the supporting leg, or else you fall. You might not literally fall down onto the floor, but every step will come with a "thud, thud, thud" that hurts your knees and scares off all the animals you might want to see while you walk. The result is that you feel heavy and clumsy.

When your weight is fully over your standing leg, on the other hand, your "swinging" leg suddenly feels much lighter. Instead of walking feeling like exercise, it becomes simply a matter of constantly shifting your body weight. You don't have to micromanage your "foot strike" or any of that business, because you no longer fall onto your foot when you walk. Instead, you're swinging your foot forwards, and then turning to bring your body weight fully onto that foot -- so that the other foot can swing effortlessly and easily. You never have a "footfall" because your body weight never falls at all.

In fact, as you bring your weight UP onto your next supporting foot, you get taller, rather than shorter. No "thud-thud-thud," but quiet footfalls that are a lot nicer to your knees.

One hand stays still, the other moves with your body.
Presto, clean fingies.

And it's a lot easier to do that when the foot that's about to swing helps you shift all of your body weight onto the other side. And that's what washing your hands in this funny way lets you do.

Shifting your weight to wash your hands — all the movement comes from the change in your body weight, not your arm muscles.

When the ball of your back foot is on the floor hand the same-side hand comes forwards, you are practicing two things:

1.   Moving from the middle of your body, rather than from your extremities

2.   Shifting your body weight back and forth from one foot to the other

This is better than half the benefit of your average tai chi program, and you can get those benefits just by washing your hands!

Turning the hips can move the hands forwards and backwards too rather than pumping the elbows.

So a small bonus! You're also improving how well you "externally" and "internally" rotate your hips. That's a lot of inside baseball we won't go into here, but the long and short of it is that shifting your balance better means that all of your joints will have an easier time changing shape, which therefore means a lot less muscular strain doing all the things you do in life.

Bonus Tip: you can also try this pushing a shopping cart or cutting vegetables at the kitchen counter. Who knew chopping a salad could make you a better dancer?

Bonus Bonus Tip: if you have tennis elbow, this will help your recovery by reducing the strain you put on your arms.

TAKING THE LOW ROAD
(TO YOUR FRIDGE)

So what's in the bottom of your fridge?

How do you check? What do you do in order to get toilet paper out of the back of your bathroom cabinet? For most of us, the answer is "stoop awkwardly while quietly bemoaning the fact that reaching under cabinets is clumsy and no fun at all for our backs."

It doesn't have to be this way.

Instead, try this: stand with your feet roughly shoulder width apart. Begin to bend your knees a little, and then straighten them out again. Every time your knees bend, notice that your ankles bend a little bit, too. So begin to bend your knees and ankles, and then go back up a couple of times. You can also feel your hips beginning to bend and then to straighten.

This is where the fun begins. Go up and down in a comfortable range of movement, just bouncing up and down a bit. When all three joints bend at the same time, it's *much easier!* And then you have a choice. Do you make your head go up and down like a pogo stick, which is work, or can you also let the ball of your foot bend along with your other leg joints, so that your head stays the same height?

When you stand in front of your refrigerator, begin folding up all these joints, by raising your heels so everything bends, and then lowering them. Try one heel and then the other, until you can "tap tap tap" with either leg, and then with both legs (remembering to minimize the "pogo stick" effect unless you want this to become a workout). Then, when you're ready, just fold up all these leg joints until you're in a high-heeled squat, and you can reach for those veggies (or toilet paper) without having to stoop. To get tall again, just set your heels down and as you do that, unfold all the joints together.

This is MUCH less work than stooping.

Easy effortless kitchen squats can be learned in just a few minutes, and by tapping your heels in front of the refrigerator, you'll stay ready to squat any time you need to. Better yet, instead of hurting your back picking up that pot of beans from the bottom of your fridge, you can just reach for it and hold it to your stomach, and *then* unfold without straining anything at all.

But wait: isn't squatting supposed to be exercise?

Sure. Squatting is great exercise...the way people teach it on Youtube. And if you did "the toilet paper squat" fifty times a day, quickly, you'd get a great workout. But that's not what we're after here. We're trying to help you grow habits which will take the effort *out* of your day, so you have more left over to do the fun things you actually *want* to do.

And that means balance.

When your weight is on your heels, you often feel more secure than when your weight is on the balls of your feet. That's why many people lock their knees (and their lower backs!): they're not comfortable having their weight forwards, so they put it back, even though it's more muscular effort. Feeling "stable" feels safer for a lot of people.

But the problem with that is that you're buying that stability at the price of mobility. Instead, once you notice that your knees and hips and ankles and feet can all bend together in a single cooperative movement, you can also include raising the heel to shift your weight forwards, so that your head and hips and toes are all roughly in a line. This makes bending a lot easier than if you did it by bending with your hips and backside *behind* the line of your head and toes. Remember washing your legs?

Balance matters!

The further your weight is from your center, the harder everything gets. And that's why getting that pot close to you when you unfold helps, too. You might be able to squat straight-armed to hold out a rubber ducky for your kid in the bathtub. But you probably wouldn't even *try* that with a twenty-pound dumbbell, even if your toddler was a Baby Superhero, unless you were already "serious athlete" levels of fit and strong.

Optimally, over time you could stand everywhere with your weight centered so that instantly squatting, or bouncing up out of a squat, becomes "a thing you do" without even having to think about it. And depending on how you use your hips, you might have the calf and ankle flexibility to keep your heels on the floor when you do it. But that's just bonus points for people who won the flexibility lottery, and more about "looking neat" than "living better."

For most of us, it's about getting the veggies, or else getting that toilet paper and then being able to pop up and get somewhere else.

Preferably quickly and easily.

SCROLLING WITH YOUR SCREEN

Phones are great. But "cellphone neck" is terrible.

You live on Planet Earth. I live <u>on my phone.</u>

Nothing feels quite like being bent over a phone for a half-hour while carrying on a text conversation or watching a show. Some people get such a bad case of "cellphone neck" that they literally begin to grow bone spurs at the back of their skulls in order to help their necks get more support. Imagine: *bunions, but for your skull.*

OUCH.

If this is sounding like you, try this: put your forearm up against a wall with your hand pointing straight up facing you, and your elbow bent at ninety degrees.

Then move your elbow up, so that your arm goes straight towards the ceiling and the angle at the inside of your elbow gets bigger. Then go back down to where you started. Then up again. Along the way, notice that the inner angle of your shoulder (armpit) also changes with it. Your shoulder and elbow are both at ninety degrees, and then the angle gets bigger and bigger on both sides until you get to a point where you can feel it starting to get harder. When you feel that, STOP. Don't make this hard – that's not what this book is about.

Instead, stay in a range of motion that's easy, and begin watching your hand as it goes up and down. But remember, your hand is just hanging out and going along for the ride, while your elbow goes up and down and your shoulder helps your elbow do that (tip: you may feel your shoulder blade going down a little when your elbow goes up, and vice versa). The better you get at having your elbow and armpit cooperate, the lighter and lighter your arm will start to feel.

As you go lower, the elbow/armpit angles get smaller

Then try it with your other hand. When you have a sense of that, try it with your hand off the wall, and let the elbow really straighten out and bend a *lot*, so long as you stay comfortable. The hand goes a ways up, and a ways down.

Then try *watching* one hand doing that while the other's held in the air. You can take turns with each hand, or have one going up while the other comes down. Whee.

What does this have to do with my neck?

A LOT. If, instead of bending over to bring your face to the phone, the way a cat or dog brings their face to a food bowl, you can *instead* bring your phone up to you, and use your other arm to scroll up and down, push buttons, what–have–you.

HOW'S IT WORK?

Remember how you moved your body when you washed your hands, and how you moved it when you washed your legs? This is the same idea, but going upwards. Your appendages are just that – appendages. In terms of your body, they're not "the main event." That's your torso with its big powerful muscles. You have as much muscle between each shoulder blade and your ribs than you do in an entire arm. So by thinking about moving your hands from the elbow and the armpit, you're teaching yourself to use chest and back muscles you may not have ever even realized you had (unless they complained).

And by doing that, you suddenly liberate strength you weren't able to use before. Your arms don't get lighter, but they *feel* lighter, because you're learning how to use your shoulders properly. By looking at your phone while it's brought up to you, rather than bending down, you also train your spine to cooperate with your shoulders in the process, and that habit will eventually help you to get looser and looser through the ribs. Not only is it a much more human and dignified way to use a phone, it's also much, much better for when you have to reach into a high cabinet or put something on top of the refrigerator.

Similarly, when you *do* look down, you'll be doing so in a way that gets more of you in action, meaning *your neck isn't stuck doing all the work.*

Like learning to sit with more ease and grace, this is primarily a case of keeping an open mind. The *habit* of bending over and hunching to look at things will initially make this seem like more effort. Muscularly, though, this is actually much easier than having your head hang down off your neck while the muscles at the top of your shoulders and the base of your skull get tighter and tighter. This new habit will pay you big dividends if you can be open-minded enough to chase it.

... also 68% less likely to bump into a coworker while reading memos at the office.

STUCK STANDING IN LINE:
THE CALL OF THE (SHOPPING) CART

So you're stuck in line. What do you do? You could check messages on your phone. You could talk to your neighbor. You could knit! (I've seen this: when you have your thread carefully spooled to emerge from your fanny pack at the grocery, you are REALLY INTO KNITTING).

What do you do WHILE you're doing that?

I tap my foot. It's a really good thing to do. Plus, depending on how you do it, you either look impatient-but-polite, which is a bonding experience at the DMV, or like you've got a really good song in your head, which makes you seem like a fun person. But you wouldn't be up to this section of this little book if you weren't wondering "I bet there's some WAY I could be tapping my feet?"

AND YOU'D BE RIGHT!

There are lots of ways that you can tap your toes while standing around bored in the grocery store. The way we're going to do it is to pay attention to the foot that ISN'T doing the tapping. Remember washing your hands to improve your walking? Same deal.

Sounds weird? Well, it is and it isn't. If you're standing around and you're on two feet, to tap one of them, you first have to do something SUPER important. you have to take your weight away from the foot that's going to be doing all the tapping, and towards the one that won't be. Otherwise, you're doing Comedic Pratfalls For the Amusement of Children (and spilling your groceries all over creation).

So first you shift your weight, then you... have to make a really hard choice. Do I lift my foot into the air to start toe-tapping, or do I leave my heel down?

For right now, let's leave the heel down. At the moment, you're what a lot of Tai Chi people call "single weighted," which is a fancy way of saying you may be getting support from both feet, but that your weight is only on one foot. (if you don't WANT support, lift your tapper all the way into the air...)

In fencing, tapping with the heel down is called an "appel." It's a "call" they used to use way back in the old days to say "okay, I'm ready, let's fence." In this case, it's your tapping toe calling your standing foot to say "hey, is my body weight over there with you?" Now, fencers do this from a pretty low and wide stance. We won't, because that's physically demanding and *how much sense would that make when you're holding a bag of groceries* or standing in front of a shopping cart? So try it. Raise your toe and tap your foot twice. Pop-pop!

Some questions to investigate while you're bored in line:

1. Did you lose your balance?

2. Did your head wobble or bob up and down?

3. Did the feel of the floor change under your supporting (non-tapping) shoe?

The goal is for all of these to eventually get to "nope." That means you might have to hold onto your shopping cart for balance.

SUPER IMPORTANT TIP

While holding onto your shopping cart, DON'T LEAN ON IT.

When you hold onto something you naturally put a little tiny amount of body weight onto an object so that you can use it for balance. That's super-helpful. But if you LEAN your body weight into it, your point of balance goes from "under your head, somewhere near your feet," to "someplace way outside your body. that forces you to tense up in order to stabilize yourself.

This is not happy shopping.

So counter-intuitively, your best balance comes when you HOLD the cart, but still rely on your legs to do all the "holding you up" bits. If you need the cart, play with how little weight you need to put onto it to stay happily upright.

WHY DOES IT WORK?

As the old saying goes, "neurons that fire together, wire together." Or, to put it a less nerdy way, practice doesn't make perfect. Practice makes PERMANENT. So if you don't feel steady when you walk, practicing your unsteady walk won't help. You'll just get *really good* at being unsteady.

To walk well, you have to balance on one foot while changing the shape of your body (you know, leg moves forward, arms swing, all that stuff). The more comfortably you can keep your weight centered over the leg touching the ground, the easier it is to take a step. (So unless you're Hop-Along Ned, you need to practice your toe-tapping skills with each foot!)

Meanwhile, your "appel" also changes the shape of your body. But it does that by keeping your heel on the ground and bringing the toe down, so it's easy and safe. The better you get at it, the more varieties of toe taps you can try, like turning your heel to tape side, then front, then side twice, then switching feet.... at which point not only are you improving your balance while you chat on the phone, but you're in a better mood, because it's really hard to stay droopy and slumped while *casually and beautifully doing half a dance routine.*

Which is really important if you really *are* doing this in the DMV and you still have 90 minutes to go before it's your turn....

BONUS QUESTION FOR SUPER MOTIVATED OR TERRIFYINGLY BORED PEOPLE!

When you tap your toe, what does the leg doing the tapping feel like? How far up your leg and into your body can you feel changes happening just because you're raising your toe and then tapping it back down?

And how can you take the lessons from "Floppy Feet" to help your legs get really, really relaxed while you do it?

BORING REPETITIVE STUFF, OR, "I GOT HIGH SCORE ON LAUNDRY!"

"Oh, God, this is SO Annoying!"

How many times have you heard or thought that?

A lot, I bet. I get it during data entry. And folding laundry. NOBODY in my house likes folding laundry. I get to skate on three other chores *and* mostly be the one who drinks the coffee rather than making it, because my wife hates folding laundry so much, she considers this a *really, REALLY good deal.* (I also kill "certain offending bugs," but you get the point. Until we train bugs to fold laundry, they're not welcome in our house).

Ffloyd found fulfillment in everyday household chores

But there's something about tedium that's really neat. Repetitive tasks can be REALLY exciting. You can enjoy folding laundry as much as my Mom loved playing Tetris.

Yes, I WAS voted "least in need of LSD" back in college, why do you ask?

Wait, What?

That's right. Tedium is exciting. Here's how it works. No, really, what I'm about to show you will take the worst chore of your life and make it totally palatable, like putting mental bacon on it.

Take some really awful, horrible, repetitive, tedious task. The sort you're doing to do, all the while your forebrain screams at you "I don't WANNA...." You'll hate doing it.

Mostly because you're letting your forebrain scream *don't wanna"* at you.

Now, here's what you're going to do. DIVE IN.

While you're doing it, pretend what you're doing is a very specific form of dance or meditation, and focus on doing it as effortlessly and efficiently as possible. Fewest mouse clicks, most effortless sweeping, fewest folds until the kid's underwear is piled neatly, whatever it is. Focus on *exactly* how you perform the movements as if you're dancing for an audience of thousands. High score on laundry.

About forty minutes in you'll notice that your pulse is up, and you're WAYYY more alert than you usually are. And when you get towards the end of your job, your pulse is really going to go up, not just a little bit, but like you were watching the COOLEST MOVIE EVER.

Like this, only with sex, football, and giant robots. And puppies. (My illustrator thinks robots are super cool. She can't wait for robots that ALSO fold laundry)

See, the reason you get bored and hate doing tedious tasks is that they don't do much for your forebrain. Your forebrain would really rather be doing something with more novelty to it. But.. you know, red paper, green stamp, blue box, rinse, repeat, rinse, repeat, Red paper, Green Stamp, Blue Box.... what's in it for Mister Forebrain? Nothing, and it knows it, so it tells Miss Amygdala, "DON'T WANNA." And Miss Amygdala responds with "I HATE this, I'm SO bored, ugh."

And then you're miserable for four hours AND did a bad job at it, too. Don't believe me?

Try making a small child clean up Legos.

But by embracing the tedium and focusing not on how stupid and robotic it is, but focusing on doing it as gracefully as possible, your forebrain goes into "I'm the boss" mode, and monitors what you're doing. Because that's what forebrains *do*. The rest of the brain could give two piddles anyway, and by the time you're done, so far as it's concerned, you just did two hours of intricate dance and are PSYCHED ABOUT LIFE. It's like a triple-espresso and a rave all rolled into one. You feel better, you LOOK better (bored looks old, and not "good old," either). Plus, you *get clean laundry.*

WHY'S IT WORK?

Because we're really smart, but our nervous systems are TOTALLY gullible.

You see, your nervous system doesn't know the difference between dancing, playing a video game, or folding laundry. It's all "repetitive precision motion" so far as your limbic system is concerned. So if you invest in really paying attention to the quality of your movements and really making them as fluid and elegant as possible, Miss Limbic System notices and goes "wait, hold on, she's paying REALLY close attention to this! This must be super cool amazing stuff! I should be emotionally invested! HEY, AMYGDALA, GET EMOTIONALLY INVESTED, THIS STUFF IS AWESOME!"

PLUS, you don't have any performance anxiety, and failure isn't really an option. So not only is there excitement, but it's excitement AND safety.

This is a place your nervous system really loves to be.

YOU CAN DO THE THING!

We believe in you.

WAIT A MINUTE... how's this going to help me be less klutzy?

Well, you just spent all that time paying really close attention to how you moved, right? Your nervous system may be gullible, but the more you pay attention to how you move, the more it starts saying things like *"adjust arm angle fourteen degrees, roger"* while you fine-tune The Dance Of A Thousand Folded Tee Shirts.

All you had to do was pay attention for forty minutes straight, or what-have-you. Which *could* completely violate the basic premise of the book, but this is a task *you have to do anyway.*

Would you rather spend forty minutes with the "I don't wannas?"

In this process, by paying very careful attention to what you're doing, you go from "the thing is terrible until I'm totally done," to "the thing has a lot of repetitive steps," and every time you finish a step, you recognize that and your brain gives you a little *DING! Check-mark of Accomplishment*, and a tiny hit of dopamine as you recognize your job well done. Those little dopamine hits help time pass by more rapidly while you work, and help you to get even more invested in doing what you're doing, so that it becomes easier and easier to let time fly by while you crank through things that you'd otherwise want to whine and moan about.

Folding laundry isn't inherently exciting. But you know, the thing is, *nothing is actually inherently exciting.* It's all about whether we consider something worth doing, or worth paying attention to, and when you pay attention to the physical movements, the "dance," as it were, your nervous system sits up and goes "okay, *I'm here for it.*"

And the nifty thing is, since everything you do requires movement, everything is potentially a little dance you can pay attention to. Nice, huh?

=========

BED: BREATHE YOUR WAY TO SLEEP. OR, "SWEET DREAMS, MARSHMALLOW HUMAN."

Little rituals are important. That's why I often forget to put my socks away in the hamper when I get home (where I prefer to be barefoot), but I ALWAYS fold them up neatly when I take them off. You've almost certainly got something like this going on -- some habit that's "so you" that your spouse has used it as a running gag for the last twenty years and even your grand-kids know about it.

Here's one to add. If the shower was the theoretical start to your day, this is the theoretical finish (at least, until the dog needs to go out).

Every part of your body is connected to every other part of your body. We know this because we don't just leave our arms behind us on the couch when we go to let the dog in, right?

No arm in trying...

Okay, so it's a little more involved than that, I admit. But the long and the short of it is that your skin and fascia (think of this as Super-powered Saran-Wrap for your muscles) wrap your body together, so any movement in one part of your body pushes, pulls, rotates, shifts, twists, or does SOMETHING to affect the rest of your body. That's why we started our day with toe wriggling, remember? A little bit of toe and foot wriggling eventually gets felt all the way up to your head.

Now for sleep. Most Americans are so sleep-deprived that a survey a few years back said that given a choice between sex and an extra hour of sleep, most of us would pick rolling over and hitting "snooze" on the alarm. So let's make a *good night' sleep*, rather than tossing and turning, the last part of your day. In the morning we set up for bouncing around. At night, we're getting set for Quality Snoozing. Let's start by getting in bed. Now lay there and breathe.

But not just any old way.

The goal is to "quiet" your neck, arms, and legs by making them feel as soft as you can possibly make them. Seriously soft and limp, like wet spaghetti noodles. No, don't worry about your back yet, it'll take care of itself. You're just a big old marshmallow.

Then, start taking big, gentle breaths, as if you wanted to fill up your whole torso with air. Now, it doesn't actually matter if you're a "chest breather," a "belly breather," or even a "BACK breather" (yes, there's such a thing). Just enjoy the weight of your body on the mattress, letting the part that's in contact stay in contact, while the rest of you fills up with air and expands, and then empties itself of air and contracts. Sort of like bread rising in the oven with every breath. Go with the intention of breathing from the tops of your shoulders all the way down to the bottoms of your hips.

A funny thing will start to happen if you do this. You'll start shedding tension. And since you're trying this out as a HABIT, you'll be getting used to blowing away your tension right before sleep. The end result is that you'll fall asleep faster and sleep better, because as soon as you start your Sleepytime Ritual, the rest of the ritual (zonk, splat, possible snoring *though we know you never do that*), will follow.

HOLD ON A MINUTE.

What's this got to do with staying looser and moving more easily?

Turns out that when you breathe like this, slowly and gradually you start to feel a bunch of peculiar and crazy things.

For instance, you might feel your forearm bones rotating or twisting one way when you inhale, and the other way when you exhale (you can spend hundreds of dollars to learn this at expensive seminars, if you'd rather do that than just focus on falling asleep). As you slowly get used to feeling new movement patterns happen, your ability to feel what happens in your body will get better and better, too. You'll stop being the kid who bangs into furniture all day and constantly drops the cups and bowls, and start being somebody who can even dance a little. Maybe somebody who even gets *asked* to dance a little.

Remember wiggling your toes? What if your legs could get so soft your ankles moved <u>because of</u> your breath?

That means you'll have a much easier time moving and doing and generally *just being*. Life will be easier, and you'll be happier.

And after all, isn't that the point?

Don't forget to breathe.

Sweet Dreams, Marshmallow Human.

ABOUT THE AUTHORS:

If you hate the book, blame Russ. If you like the art, credit Kat.

Russ Mitchell used to be terrifyingly clumsy and spent a long time sad and depressed because he was Mister Failboat and always picked last for sports. After years and years, he got a lot less clumsy and found out that he really likes helping other people feel more balanced, confident, and capable using this super-powered way of paying attention to yourself called "the Feldenkrais Method." (It's okay, you don't have to pronounce it) He can be reached at russ@irvingfeldenkrais.com

Kat Laurange will draw on any piece of paper that stands still long enough, a survival skill that served her well in school. When she's not drawing, she's drinking coffee, chasing the kids, writing stories, and swinging swords at people (don't worry, they like it, and usually they block), and drinking more coffee, near Dallas, Tx. Her petition to extend the day to 36 hours has yet to be approved by the government.. Kat likes helping people with fun projects; find her at katlaurange.carrd.co

CPSIA information can be obtained
at www.ICGtesting.com
Printed in the USA
LVHW052007150623
749895LV00003B/272

9 798394 146640